Four the Love of Family

"Brooklyn 5.0"

LINDA BERRY

BOOK 4

BOOK 4 IN THE SERIES BROOKLYN 5.0

To order additional copies of this book, contact:
Xlibris
844-714-8691
www.Xlibris.com
Orders@Xlibris.com

ISBN: Softcover   979-8-3694-3185-6
        EBook   979-8-3694-3186-3

Print information available on the last page

Rev. date: 11/04/2024

Table of Contents

Introduction

At a minimum, a four-year-old child can recognize close family members. Immediate family members consist of One's siblings, parents, spouse, and grandparents. Recognition is repetitive at family gatherings. According to Oxford languages, recognition is acknowledgement of existence, validity, or legality. For the purposes of this production, formal recognition can be diplomatic in the life of a four-year-old. Cognitive skills are developed as sight and repetition are applied. In this version Brooklyn parents are having a baby. Willow is the new addition. Willow is baking in mommy's oven. When the baby is done, it comes out of the mommy oven. Knowing parents and grandparents are part of a loving family. Brooklyn's immediate family will be introduced as part of the growing family tree. Let's see how family is part of Brooklyn's family tree. At the bottom of the tree is Brooklyn and her sister. Next layer is her parents. Next layer is her parents' siblings. The last layer will be her grandparents.

Presenting baby Willow

Brooklyn can articulate that something is growing in mommy's stomach. She asks her other Ashley "what is that mommy?" as she points to her mother's stomach. Ashley exclaims as she smiles very brightly "I am baking your sibling in the oven". "It is not done yet". In the meantime, Ashley is preparing for the new arrival of the lastest addition of the family.

With all the excitement Brooklyn saw her Dad take her mom to the hospital. Brooklyn had to stay at home. Finally the new arrival of baby Willow has arrived. Brooklyn went to the hospital to see her new sibling. Finally the wait is over. Baby Willow was finsihed baking and out of the oven. They were a bigger happy family. Once they got home the family was able to sit together. Brooklyn has a little sister - Willow. More important Brooklyn is a big sister now.

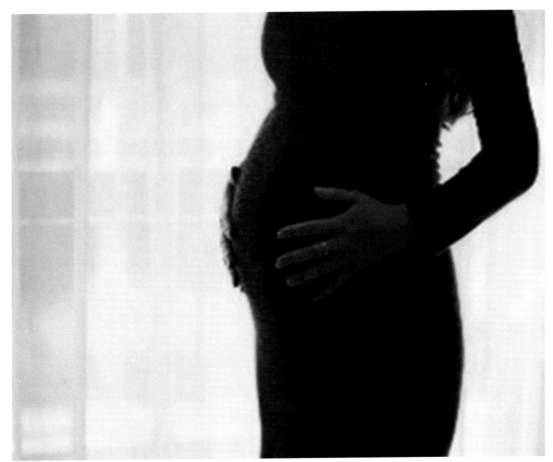

Parents

In contrast; One day Brooklyn was riding in her car seat in Granny Sitas car. Brooklyn said Granny Sita I have parents. My parents are smart. Granny Sita exclaimed "You are smart too Brooklyn. Brooklyn smiled. Brooklyn further stated My parents have Parents. Do you have parents? Granny Sita looked through mirror to see Brooklyn in the rear car seat and said yes, I have parents. They both live in heaven now. Brooklyn had a visual of her parents. Brooklyn Parents real name are Ashely and Garey Berry, II.

Brooklyn had a vision of Ashleys parents. She call Ashleys mom Nana and Ashleys dad Papa. Their real names are Regina and Kevin Dansby

In the meantime, Ashley is preparing for the new arrival of the lastest addition of the family.

With all the excitement Brooklyn saw her Dad take her mom to the hospital. Brooklyn had to stay at home. Finally the new arrival of baby Willow. Brooklyn went to the hospital to see her new sibling. Finally the wait is over. Baby Willow was finsihed baking and out of the oven. They were a bigger happy family. Once they got home the family was able to sit together. Brooklyn has a little sister - Willow. More important Brooklyn is a big sister now.

Aunts and Uncles

Brooklyn has parents. Her parents are Ashley and Garey(Goldie) Berry.

Ashley has siblings. Ashleys siblings are: Nikita(Nikki). Heather, Eboney Joshua and Jeremy.

Garey siblings are Linda and Tommie.

Ashley and Garey siblings are Brooklyn's Aunts and Uncles.
Brooklyn know all her immdeiate family members such as aunts and uncles.

Grand Parents

Brooklyn has another set of grandparents. Granny Sita and Grandpa George. Their real names are Linda and George Mason. They are married. Brooklyn is the flower girl in their wedding. The big lesson for children to learn Is when a marriage takes place, the family grows. Brooklyn know that one of her other set of grandparents are Granny Sita and Grandpa George.

At a minum a four year old child may know her sibling(s), parents, grandpaents, aunts and uncles. Garey father name is Garey Berry. Brooklyn oldest grandparent are Judy and Tommie Berry. They are in their 90s. The cousins were not forgotten. The cousins were left out on purpose to focus on immediate family. Stay tuned to book five to meet some of brooklyns cousins. Brooklyn can recognize and say all her immediate family name.

About the Author

Linda Berry has published a book prior to this series. The author graduated from Ashland University a B.S. in Criminal Justice Administration. While at Ashland she became the president of her sorority Delta Sigma Theta, Sorority Inc. Her master's degree is from Tiffin University in Criminal Justice/Homeland Security. She completed doctoral courses at North Central University. Linda Retired from the State of Ohio working for both the Adult Parole Authority in Cleveland, Ohio and the Department of Developmental Disabilities in Columbus, Ohio. Ms. Bery retired from the Army National Guard as a Military Police head of Operations.

Linda's volunteer work is Extensive. She gardens at the Franklin Park Conservatory in Columbus, as well as a lifetime member and Service Officer for the Veterans of Foreign War. She is a lifetime member of the VFW, American Legion, and Disenabled American Veterans. Before the pandemic Linda worked as a substitute teacher in Reynoldsburg, Ohio. She is a member of the Broad Street Presbyterian Church in Columbus, Ohio. Attends a church called the Atlanta Methodist Church in New Holland, Ohio and cooks for the Living Waters Church in Williamsport Ohio. Linda enjoys Traveling.

She is the founder and philanthropist of Excalibur, LLC, since 1990, in Cleveland and Columbus, Ohio. Excalibur, LLC is a non-profit organization dedicated to helping at risk youth stay engaged: and employed through church activities, horticulture, helping people move and catering. The youth work all year round whenever the opportunity presents itself. Overall. Linda enjoys Traveling.

I-den-ti-TEA

When you start off having tea, you grow up appreciating tea.
You can identify with tea. Exposure is the key.

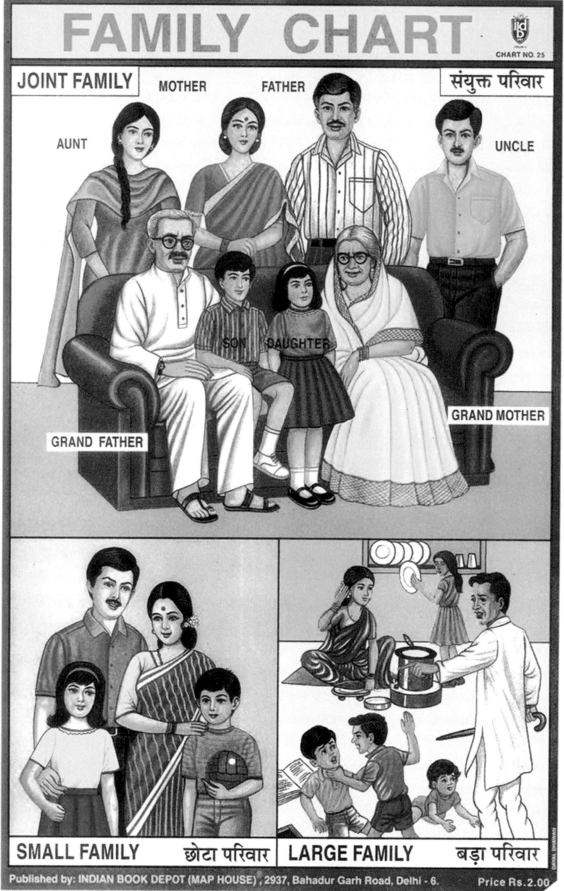

FAMILY CHART

CHART NO. 25

JOINT FAMILY

MOTHER   FATHER

संयुक्त परिवार

AUNT

UNCLE

SON   DAUGHTER

GRAND FATHER

GRAND MOTHER

SMALL FAMILY   छोटा परिवार   LARGE FAMILY   बड़ा परिवार

Published by: INDIAN BOOK DEPOT (MAP HOUSE), 2937, Bahadur Garh Road, Delhi - 6.   Price Rs.2.00

E-mail ibdmaps@ndb.vsnl.net.in   Printed at : Vikas Enter

Printed in the United States
by Baker & Taylor Publisher Services